# Psalms of My Soul

## By

## Kalita Hodges Allen

Printed in the United States of America.

First printing, 2022.

All works are original.

# Psalms of My Soul

Kalita Hodges
Allen

# Table of Contents

ODE TO MY FATHER

KEEP GOING  Haiku

ODE TO EAGLES

THE MIGHTY ABORIGINALS

BIRTHING GREATNESS

SONG OF SAINTED SOULS

ABBA YOU ARE MY
EVERYTHING

GRATEFULNESS

I WILL ALWAYS LOVE YOU

FOR THE EAGLE

A DISPARAGE OF MARRIAGE

# ODE TO MY FATHER

ABBA Father, YOU inspire me to
BE!

To exist in time and place,

And to walk in the existence

Of whom YOU designed me to BE.


To do of Your good pleasure

Whatever Thou will.

To honor YOU in service

With all my skills.


It is a pleasure

And the pleasure is mine,

To humbly work for YOU

In this moment in time.

Kalita Hodges
Allen

Appointed for the anointment.

Anointed for the appointment.

Wherever YOU say go

Is what I will do!

Kalita Hodges Allen

# KEEP GOING

## Haiku

Got to keep going!

'Tis the only way for me

There's no turning back.


Kalita Hodges Allen

# ODE TO EAGLES

The best thing that you can do

is go on 'head and be your best self.

Do not settle for nothing less.

Realize and recognize that they

were only part of your test.

They were sent to try you with fire.

They were sent to stop you from your
goal.

The things they did worked together
for your good.

The things they did proved you gold.

So dust yourself from the ashes

of what was never meant for you,

Fly high above the mess of their
regret,

and do what Eagles do!

Kalita Hodges
Allen

Give GOD all the pieces

of everything that is left.

Tell yourself you are ready now

to take you off the shelf.

No more mental anguish.

No more abuse and sore.

It is time for you to spread your
wings.

It is time for you to soar!

Kalita Hodges Allen

# THE MIGHTY ABORIGINALS

There must be something special
about you

if they would lie and change your
name.

There must be something special
about you

if they would hide from where you
came.

Then wrote their lies on paper

while their laws gave them protection;

Then stole the land from under your
feet

and lightened your complexion.

Then paid another nation

to pretend that they were you.

Then dumbed down your ancestors,

and changed your language too.

All of this was done

to erase the real Originals.

There's something mighty special

about the native Aboriginals!

You ever wondered why

they chopped off all the noses?

They did not want you to see yourself,

so, they chopped off all the noses.

Turned you against your woman,

but she is good enough for them.

Of a kind, they know she is first,

but they tricked you to condemn.

Now you are chasing what

is not original anymore,

but what's fake and plastic,

And full of fillers galore.

They know that she is special.

They know she is a Queen.

They know she is the one

That gives birth to the Kings

We are all Henriettas.

We've all suffered lacks.

Copper colored coming out the fire.

Though weapons formed,

We are still intact.

Kalita Hodges Allen

# BIRTHING GREATNESS

I know there is Greatness

bursting forth from me!

Mixed with it is purpose.

They have come to set me free.


Free to live my best life!

Free to live one blessed!

They have come to barren land,

to move me from this mess.

Kalita Hodges
Allen

I am so glad to see them!

I am so glad they came!

From the moment that they adopted
me,

my life will never be the same.


They gave me their bond word

that this was not a game.

To prove their loyalty to me,

they gave me both their names.

Now my works will follow me

both here and in life beyond.

They helped me to birth a legacy.

ABBA YAH thy will be done!


Because I wrote the vision,

It did come to pass.

Greatness has reached out for me,

and I Am no more last.

Purpose has enveloped me,

and I Am no more last.

Kalita Hodges Allen

# SONG OF SAINTED SOULS

Though trials and troubles may come,

the Just shall live by faith.

All of it worked together for your good.

There is nothing going to waste.


HE has great plans for you.

Abundant life and so much more.

No man can stop your destiny

when GOD opens up the door.

HE knows HIS plans for you.

Plans of peace and not of evil.

Put your trust in HIM and believe,

And know that HE is able.


Help me make right decisions

in seasons I must choose,

for when YOU order and guide my
steps,

I know I will not lose.

Help me not to doubt O' LORD,

and not to be afraid.

You know the plans You have for me.

My path already made.


Fearfully and wonderfully made I am!

I Am whose hands did mold.

My destiny I trust with You,

'til home on streets of gold.

Kalita Hodges Allen

# ABBA FATHER, YOU ARE MY EVERYTHING

Thank you LORD

for the wind on my skin.

Your strength in my back.

The cover of Your wings

when I am under attack.


The thirst that You quench

deep down in my soul.

My life's in Your hands.

My future You hold.

For blessings of grandeur.

For blessings thought small.

For giving me your promises,

and the greatest gift of all.


Though struggles come daily,

this one thing I know.

You are always there for me,

and will never leave me alone.


Let GOD be true,

and every man a liar.

I'll stand firm on Your word

when tried by the fire.


Kalita Hodges
Allen

LORD, I know You are with me.

You have never left my side.

You never sleep or slumber,

and know every tear I have cried.


Words don't give You justice

as much as actions do.

I thank You for Your love for me,

so honest and so true!


Thank You for my journey,

and all that it contains.

Through ups and downs, You have
given me

joy and peace I cannot explain.

Your life you gave freely.

My life, I give back.

Swing down o'sweet chariot!

No turning back, no turning back.


My soul yells Victory King Yeshua!

I proclaim it, and loud.

Will keep fighting my LORD,

'til I see You in the clouds.

Kalita Hodges Allen

# GRATEFULNESS

I thank You for the opportunity of my
view right now,

to bask in the beauty of Your flowers

surrounded and enhanced by Your
Creation ...

The way they shimmer and dance

with each soft whisper of wind.

It is as if they hear their own song.

O' Father, play it again!

The showmanship of Your artwork

is nothing short of exquisite,

and I am blessed and honored to be

 in attendance of Your exhibit.

I am not trying to be poetic,

but Your splendor stirs something
inside of me.

The new things do spring forth!

I feel it inside of me!

Kalita Hodges Allen

# I WILL ALWAYS LOVE YOU

## A Poem for My Children

I will always love you baby

through the trials and through the
storms,

and pray to GOD for you,

to protect you from all harm.


I know you are all grown up

and think you know it all.

Don't say Moma did not tell you,

pride comes before a fall.

Kalita Hodges
Allen

The strong and black woman I am

may want to wring your neck.

The brave Queen Mother I am,

and faith keeps me in check


You need to check yo'self

'Fo you wreck yo'self.

Though brash my love, it's true.

Just hear the words I am saying,

Then decide and do what you choose.


Just remember I am older and wiser.

I have seen it all before.

Don't speak everything you think

Don't walk across all floors.


Kalita Hodges
Allen

In other words, I am saying,

Think before you speak.

Not everyone has good intents,

so be careful where you eat.


Don't burn down all your bridges,

'cause some you will cross again,

I will leave the light on for you,

Until we meet again.

Kalita Hodges Allen

# FOR THE EAGLE

Still can't believe you're not here

and yet another day has passed,

that I could not touch your face,

and could not make you laugh.

It is not always easy,

I am not going to lie,

to think of memories of you

And not begin to cry.

Do not misunderstand me.

I am happy you are free,

and present with the LORD

for all eternity.

Kalita Hodges
Allen

I will always recall your strength.

GOD knows you were so brave,

and the testimony you leave behind

shall live beyond the grave.

I taught you not to give up,

and you lived up to your name.

Even though I miss you so,

I promise to do the same.

May GOD watch between me and thee

and comfort me through this pain.

Rest in power, as I go forth,

until we meet again.


Kalita Hodges Allen

# A DISPARAGE OF MARRIAGE

A lot of us married the wrong person.

That's why we're having all that pain.

Some ABBA did join together, some
He did not.

We joined that marriage on our own
free will

Because we did not want to be alone.

We thought we were too old not to be.

We wanted the wedding with the bells
and whistles,

Not realizing it came bow tied with
heartache and thistles.

Some of us let him "milk the cow"
before the marriage,

And here came the calf, so we thought
"This must be him."

Want to do the right thing,

 'Cept now this thing just can't seem
to get right.

Now we are hurting.

Wounded by what was, what we
thought.

It was so right! ...

Afraid to admit that we ignored the
warning signs.

Remember the signs? The first time
he or she crossed the line?

That was our heads up, but we didn't
let up,

Because we wanted that ring,

That from the looks of, is the only
thing solid.

Now we are left holding the ring and
the "thing,"

Because it is like our marriage had a
miscarriage.

There is hope and light at the end of
this tunnel.

To get there, all you need is two legs
to stand,

Or two knees to crawl, and two eyes
to look towards the hills,

Because that is where our help will be
a' coming;

And a broken heart filled with pieces
of hope.

Be encouraged because no matter if we walk through,

or crawl through this tunnel, guess what...

At least we are moving!


Author Kalita Hodges Allen

It is my prayer that these prophetic poems and songs speak to and uplift your spirit like they have mine. Each individual poem or song was birthed during different seasons of my life, whether it was a season of joy and worship, to a season of loss and grief. No matter what season I was in, I am fortunate enough to see that nothing has gone or will go to waste, because GOD has, and is using it all for my good.

The same applies to you if you are His child and have accepted the LORD Yeshua as your LORD and Savior. I am a witness that no matter what you are going through, or may be facing today, know this one thing that is a sure thing...There is nothing too hard for GOD. Nothing. You name it and the MOST HIGH, true and living GOD can fix it.

I urge you today to surrender it all to Him and trust Him to work on your behalf.

If you have not surrendered your heart to GOD and would like to, but don't know how, here is some help. All it takes is a sincere heart and communication with ABBA Father. This is called prayer. No need for long drawn-out prayers, but it can be simple, just so as you are honest and sincere. It is an honor to welcome you with an invitation to this prayer, and introduction to Our Father and His Son Yeshua the Christ, whom we call Jesus.

Father, I come to you ready to surrender my ways for Yours. I am tired and I am a sinner. I believe that Your word came in the flesh and was mortally wounded for my sins and

that His blood washed my sins away.
I ask You to forgive me for
everything, and I welcome Your
precious Lamb to live in my heart.
Thank You for saving me from me. In
the name of Yeshua/Jesus Christ of
Nazareth. Amen.

If you prayed this prayer,
welcome to the family of the Living
GOD. I pray you are continuously
blessed from glory to glory and filled
with His precious Holy Spirit.

May the seeds of life and hope from this collection of words plant in the good ground of your soul.

Until we meet again.